ESSENTIAL DK

COMMU
CLEARLY

ROBERT HELLER

DORLING KINDERSLEY
London • New York • Sydney • Moscow

A DORLING KINDERSLEY BOOK

Project Editors Marian Broderick,
Nicky Thompson
Project Art Editor Elaine C. Monaghan
Designers Simon J. M. Oon, Adam Powers

DTP Designer Jason Little
Production Controllers Silvia La Greca,
Michelle Thomas

Series Editor Jane Simmonds
Series Art Editor Tracy Hambleton-Miles

Managing Editor Stephanie Jackson
Managing Art Editor Nigel Duffield

First published in Great Britain in 1998
by Dorling Kindersley Limited,
9 Henrietta Street,
London WC2E 8PS

4 6 8 10 9 7 5

Copyright © 1998
Dorling Kindersley Limited, London
Text copyright © 1998 Robert Heller

Visit us on the World Wide Web at
http://www.dk.com

A CIP catalogue record for this book is available
from the British Library

ISBN 0 7513 0630 4

Reproduced by Colourscan, Singapore
Printed in Hong Kong by Wing King Tong Co. Ltd.

CONTENTS

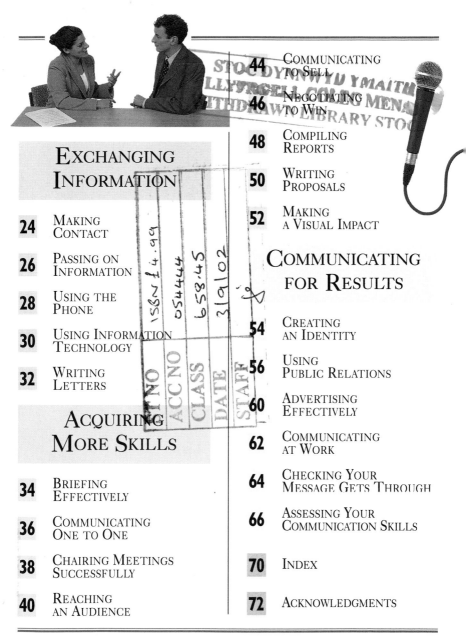

INTRODUCTION

The art of getting your message across effectively is a vital part of being a successful manager. Whether you want to make presentations with confidence or to negotiate with ease, Communicate Clearly will help you to improve your communication skills. From understanding body language to writing reports and proposals – all the key aspects of business communication are clearly explained. Also included is practical advice on using public relations, advertising, information technology, and media techniques, while 101 concise tips scattered throughout the book give further vital information. Finally, a self-assessment exercise allows you to evaluate how good you are at communicating. As you begin to communicate more effectively, this book will help you to consolidate and build on your new skills.

LEARNING THE BASICS

Everybody communicates in one way or another, but few managers deliver their messages as well as they can. Learn some basic rules to help you get your message across clearly.

WORKING TOWARDS BETTER COMMUNICATION

Good communication is the lifeblood of organizations. It takes many forms, such as speaking, writing, and listening, though its purpose is always to convey a message to recipients. Use it to handle information and improve relationships.

 1 Encourage your company to improve all types of communication.

2 Note that good communicators make much better managers.

BEING EFFECTIVE

Effective communication (and therefore effective business) hinges on people understanding your meaning, and replying in terms that move the exchange forward – preferably in the direction you would like it to go. Communicating is always a two-way process. In management, you communicate to get things done, pass on and obtain information, reach decisions, achieve joint understanding, and develop relationships.

RECOGNIZING BARRIERS

There are always at least two parties involved in any communication, each of whom may have different wants, needs, and attitudes. These wants and needs can present barriers if they conflict with those of the other party, and such barriers may stop you conveying or receiving the right message. Any communication must overcome such barriers if it is to be successful, and the first step is to recognize that they exist.

▼ **COMMUNICATING POSITIVELY**
Breaking down barriers is one of the first steps towards good communication. Maintaining eye contact, listening to what the other person is saying, and mirroring body language all help you to communicate successfully.

Facing person you are talking to shows you are not afraid to listen to what is said

Tilting your head slightly shows you are listening

Maintain eye contact with other person

Break down barriers by adopting other person's pose and actions

ACHIEVING CLARITY

The three rules that govern good communication are all associated with clarity:
● Be clear in your own mind about what you want to communicate;
● Deliver the message succinctly;
● Ensure that the message has been clearly and correctly understood.
Good communication means saying what you mean – and fully comprehending any feedback.

3 Be non-judgmental when trying to overcome other people's barriers.

CHOOSING A METHOD

It is essential when communicating a message that you give serious thought to the medium you choose. For many, this choice is often between the spoken and the written word. If you decide that you want speed and convenience, you may well choose speech as the best form of communication. Alternatively you may want something more permanent and orderly – a typed document, for example – which will attract a considered reply.

Electronic media have generated even more possibilities by creating a hybrid form of speech and writing. Thus e-mails have the speed and informality of a phone conversation, yet they are in letter form and can be filed. The purpose of the message will dictate which method to choose. Decide on your message first: then select the best method to convey it, making sure that you have mastered its technique.

CULTURAL DIFFERENCES

Communication styles in word and gesture vary as much as national cuisines. Japanese and other Asians find it easier than Europeans to be silent. The Germans, Nordics, and British, less voluble than the Latin nations, are also more restrained in gesture. The British tend to avoid saying what they mean, while Australians may disconcert others by forcefully saying exactly what they mean. Americans like communicating via rallies and slogans with strong use of visuals.

4 Match your medium to your message with great care.

COMBINING METHODS

Methods of communication can be grouped into five main types: the written word, the spoken (and heard) word, the symbolic gesture, the visual image, and a combination of these. Though the first four methods work well individually, it is now known that using two or more different communication methods together increases interest, comprehension, and retention. Methods are more potent when combined with others.

Examples of a combined approach include communicating via commercial media and electronic technology, such as multimedia and video conferencing. Multimedia allows better use of visual elements, and is increasingly the medium of choice when it comes to communicating with large numbers of people, especially employees in a big organization.

5 Wherever possible, use visuals to communicate.

Choosing Methods of Communication

Type of Communication	Examples	Usefulness
Written Word In any language and in various media, the written word is basic to literate societies.	Letters, memos, reports, proposals, notes, contracts, summaries, agendas, notices, regulations, minutes, plans, discussion documents.	The written word is the basis of organizational communication, and is used because it is relatively permanent and accessible.
Spoken Word Communication that is effective only when it is heard by the right people.	Conversations, interviews, meetings, phone calls, debates, requests, debriefings, announcements, speeches.	Verbal exchanges in person and by phone are used because of their immediacy; they are the chief means by which organizations work on a day-to-day basis.
Symbolic Gestures Any positive or negative behaviour that can be seen or heard by the intended target.	Gestures, facial expressions, actions, deeds, tone of voice, silence, stance, posture, movement, immobility, presence, absence.	Actions and body language profoundly but unconsciously affect people – propaganda depends on the manipulation of positive and negative signs.
Visual Images Images that can be perceived by a target group.	Photographs (slides and prints), paintings, drawings, illustrations, graphics, cartoons, charts, videos, logos, film, doodles, collages, colour schemes.	Visual images are used because they convey powerful conscious and unconscious messages.
Multimedia A combination of the different methods above, often involving IT (information technology).	Television, newspapers, magazines, leaflets, booklets, flyers, posters, Internet, intranet, World Wide Web, video, radio, cassettes, CD-ROMs.	Media are especially useful when they can be participative. The more professional the use of multimedia, the more effective and productive they are likely to be.

UNDERSTANDING BODY LANGUAGE

Your body language – a huge range of unconscious physical movements – can either strengthen communication or damage it. Even if you are sitting completely still, you may be unknowingly communicating a powerful message about your real feelings.

6 When standing with people, leave a personal space of about 1 m (3 ft).

COMMUNICATING ▼ BY BODY LANGUAGE

Posture is all-important in body language. On a first meeting, these three postures would create very different impressions. The positive posture might have the best effect on the outcome by encouraging open communication, while the negative one would make communication difficult.

READING BODY LANGUAGE

Because of its subtlety and range, body language is difficult to read – and to control. However, a broad understanding of body language is one route to understanding the real opinions of others. For instance, if people are inwardly feeling uncomfortable because they are lying, their awkward body language will betray the lie.

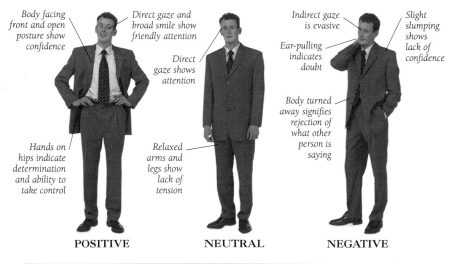

Body facing front and open posture show confidence

Direct gaze and broad smile show friendly attention

Direct gaze shows attention

Indirect gaze is evasive

Ear-pulling indicates doubt

Slight slumping shows lack of confidence

Body turned away signifies rejection of what other person is saying

Hands on hips indicate determination and ability to take control

Relaxed arms and legs show lack of tension

POSITIVE　　　　**NEUTRAL**　　　　**NEGATIVE**

CONQUERING NERVES

The nervousness people feel before making a presentation or attending an interview is very natural. Their minds prepare them for action via their nervous system, so nervousness is due in part to glands pumping the hormone adrenaline into their blood. Use body language to appear more confident than you feel by making a conscious effort to smile and to relax your arms. Look people in the eye while you are talking or listening to them, keep your posture comfortably straight, and do not fiddle with your hands.

7 Take a slow, deep breath to relax yourself, if you are feeling tense.

CULTURAL DIFFERENCES

Britons and Americans tend to leave more personal space around them than other nationalities, and are more likely to move away if they feel that their space is being invaded. People who live in rural areas may also stand further apart than city dwellers.

KEEPING YOUR DISTANCE

Leaving an acceptable distance between people is part of body language, and this distance changes depending on situation. For instance, guests at a social gathering stand closer to each other than strangers in a non-social situation. Always take care not to intrude into another's personal territory in case you arouse defensive or hostile reactions.

CREATING AN IMPRESSION

First impressions are very important. It is thought that the initial five seconds of any first meeting are more important than the next five minutes, so attention to detail can make a huge difference. Think about grooming and appropriate clothing, and err on the conservative side. Even if an informal look is required, ensure your garments and shoes are in impeccable condition. Before going into a meeting, check your appearance in a mirror to make sure that your hair is tidy.

MAKING AN IMPACT ▶
Grooming and posture always create an impression. This woman looks much more confident and capable when she has made an effort to smarten her appearance.

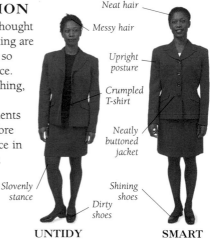

Neat hair
Messy hair
Upright posture
Crumpled T-shirt
Neatly buttoned jacket
Slovenly stance
Shining shoes
Dirty shoes

UNTIDY   **SMART**

11

UNDERSTANDING AND USING GESTURES

G*estures, together with other non-verbal communication such as posture and facial expressions, are an important part of body language. Knowing how to gesture for effect, on public platforms or in face-to-face meetings, will help to convey your message.*

8 If you are not sure how to behave abroad, ask the locals for guidance.

9 Make sure you are not unintentionally wearing a hostile expression.

CULTURAL DIFFERENCES

The non-verbal language of gestures varies from country to country. Some to watch for include the North American thumb and forefinger gesture for OK (may insult a Dane); pointing with a finger (considered rude in China); the French enthusiasm for shaking hands (excessive to Britons); shaking your head meaning "no" (means "yes" to Indians); and hugging in public (unacceptable in Singapore).

RECOGNIZING GESTURES

All skilled public speakers use gestures for emphasis. For example, John F. Kennedy used a chopping motion, while Hitler shook his fist. Devices like smacking your fist into an open palm, pointing, or spreading your palms can all reinforce points you make verbally. Remember that over-assertive gestures, such as banging a table, or other signs of anger, can alienate people. Also, if you do bang a table, take care not to drown your words.

Single gestures may combine to form complex patterns. For instance, in a private meeting, you may recognize that a colleague is appraising you while listening to you, by the position of their fingers on their cheek or chin. However, to know whether the appraisal is positive or negative, you need to observe other signs, such as whether their legs are crossed defensively, or if their head and chin are lowered aggressively.

10 Practise a range of gestures in front of a mirror to find those that look natural for you.

GIVING BODY SIGNALS

Supportive gestures, such as making eye contact and nodding while somebody is talking, create empathy – unless the person to whom you are speaking can tell that you are concealing your true feelings. Everyone can control their body language to an extent, but not totally. Choose your words with care, being as honest as possible, otherwise your body language may contradict you.

Gesturing with your hand adds emphasis

Hand on chin indicates appraisal

Raised eyebrows indicate interest

▲ LISTENING WITH APPROVAL
Approving listening is shown here by the slight tilt of the head together with friendly eye contact.

▲ PAYING ATTENTION
Eyes making contact and the body leaning forward show alertness and readiness to assist the speaker.

▲ EMPHASIZING A POINT
Using a hand to gesture emphatically is one way of reinforcing a verbal point.

Indirect gaze adds to sense of uncertainty

Arm wrapped around body is a form of self-comfort

Knitted brow and closed eyes show doubt

▲ SHOWING UNCERTAINTY
Pen-biting is a throwback to the need to be nursed. This shows fear and a lack of confidence.

▲ NEEDING REASSURANCE
One hand around the neck and the other around the waist show a need for reassurance.

▲ EXPERIENCING CONFLICT
The closed eyes and nose-pinching reveal inner confusion and conflict about what is being heard.

LEARNING TO LISTEN

The two-way nature of communication – so that both sides understand each other – is widely ignored. Listening techniques are vital, since how you listen conveys meaning to the other person and helps to make the exchange successful.

 11 Know which questions to ask – it will help you get the right answers.

SHOWING ATTENTIVENESS

When you are in search of information, consensus, or a working relationship, the more obviously you listen attentively, the better. You may need to speak to get a response, but show you do not wish to dominate the conversation. Ask open questions, which lead to discussion, and keep your responses brief. Repeat key words silently as you hear them to help you to remember what is said.

 12 Use silence confidently as a tool to encourage hesitant speakers.

USING LISTENING SKILLS

TYPE OF LISTENING	PUTTING METHODS INTO PRACTICE
EMPATHIZING Drawing out the speaker and getting information in a supportive, helpful way.	Empathize by imagining yourself in the other person's position, trying to understand what they are thinking, and letting them feel comfortable – possibly by relating to their emotional experiences. Pay close attention to what the person is saying, talk very little, and use encouraging nods and words.
ANALYZING Seeking concrete information and trying to disentangle fact from emotion.	Use analytical questions to discover the reasons behind the speaker's statements, especially if you need to understand a sequence of facts or thoughts. Ask questions carefully, so you can pick up clues from the answers and use the person's responses to help you form your next set of questions.
SYNTHESIZING Proactively guiding the exchange towards an objective.	If you need to achieve a desired result, make statements to which others can respond with ideas. Listen and give your answers to others' remarks in a way that suggests which ideas can be enacted and how they might be implemented. Alternatively, include a different solution in your next question.

- Confidence is inspired in a speaker if you listen intently.
- What you are told should be regarded as trustworthy until proved otherwise.
- Misunderstandings are caused by wishful listening – hearing only what you want to hear.
- Constant interruptions can be very off-putting for people who find it difficult to get across their point of view.

INTERPRETING DIALOGUE

Take statements at face value without reading hidden meanings into what is being said. Test your understanding by rephrasing statements and repeating them to the speaker. It should then be clear that you have understood each other – or they may correct you and clarify their statement. However, watch for physical signs, such as evasive eye contact, and verbal signs, such as hesitation or contradiction, that provide clues to the truthfulness of the message. Be careful not to hear only what you want to hear and nothing else.

USING NEURO-LINGUISTIC PROGRAMMING (NLP)

One basic theory behind neuro-linguistic programming (NLP) is that the way in which people speak shows how they think. Thinking preferences can be categorized by choice of phrase. Categories include the visual, which is indicated by phrases such as "I see where you're coming from", and the auditory, indicated by phrases such as "This sounds like a problem to me". By listening attentively, you can harmonize a conversation by "mirroring". That is, you can reply to visual language with visual, auditory with auditory, and so on. This all helps you to establish rapport with the other person. At the same time as listening intently and mirroring thinking preferences, you can also physically mirror the person. Adopting a similar posture and using the same gestures can create empathy.

Lightly clasped hands

Direct eye contact

Closed-mouth smile

Attentive posture

▲ LISTENING AND MIRRORING

NLP techniques can be used to take the tension out of a situation. For example, if you strongly disagree with someone seated opposite you, listen to them speaking, then speak yourself, using similar imagery and phraseology. If they are sitting defensively, subtly mirror their posture, then slowly change it into a more open one, as above, to encourage them to be less defensive.

RECOGNIZING PREJUDICE

When what you see or hear only fulfils your own expectations, you probably have an inflexible mind-set. Most people have this problem and are unconsciously influenced by stereotypical views. We are also influenced by others, and often adopt their opinions without thinking. Prejudices block good communication. If you can recognize your prejudiced ideas, you will be a better listener.

13 Think about the words you hear, not the person saying them.

OVERCOMING PREJUDICE

Personal prejudices may be difficult to eradicate because they are in-built and exist regardless of the behaviour or character of other people. A frequent mistake is to assume that you know what someone is going to say, and not to listen to the actual message. However, people do not always behave according to stereotype or expectation. Listen very carefully to what people are saying to you and do not let your prejudices get in the way.

AVOIDING ▼ FAVOURITISM

In this example, a manager is asking three subordinates for their views on a new strategy. He has personal prejudices about each of them. So, if the meeting is to be successful, he must overcome these prejudices and listen to what they are saying without making assumptions.

Manager has several preconceived opinions

Open-necked shirt not considered appropriate by manager

Confident woman causes manager to act defensively

Clothing mirrors what manager is wearing and gains approval

CHECKING YOU UNDERSTAND THE MESSAGE

Use phrases such as these when you need to clarify what has been said, or if you think that your own message might have been misunderstood. Take responsibility for finding out the things you need to know, and listen to the answers you are given.

66 *I'm afraid I didn't quite catch what you said. Would you mind repeating it, please?* 99

66 *I'm aware that this isn't your field, but I would be very interested to hear your opinion.* 99

66 *I can't have explained myself clearly. What I meant to establish was...* 99

RESPONDING TO SOMEONE

14 Keep an open mind about what people say.

The first step in responding to what you hear is to listen properly. If you are preparing an answer or are thinking about what to say next while you should be listening, you are not giving your full attention to what is being said. In your response, outline what you have understood so far. If you need repetition, further explanation, or extra information, do not hesitate to ask for it.

 Listen **Respond** **Act**

ACTING ON WHAT YOU HEAR

In some cases, communication is an end in itself – an update on progress, for example. In others, action is vital – clearing a bottleneck, say. What you must never do is promise an action and fail to deliver. A classic example is the employee attitude survey, which always raises expectations of action to remedy management errors. Failure to act on the survey findings means you have not listened and instead delivers a harmful message. Keep your promises – and take action as soon as possible.

▲ **LISTENING FIRST**
The three steps to successful communication are: listen carefully to what is said; respond (if necessary, ask for clarification); finally, take action.

15 Put promises in writing as soon as you can to avoid misunderstandings.

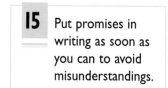

ASKING QUESTIONS

How you ask questions is very important in establishing a basis for good communication. Why, what, how, and when are very powerful words. Use them often to seek, either from yourself or from others, the answers needed to manage effectively.

 16 Ask a specific question if you want to hear a specific answer.

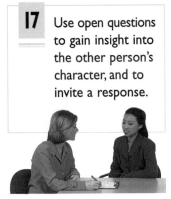

 17 Use open questions to gain insight into the other person's character, and to invite a response.

KNOWING WHAT TO ASK

The right questions open the door to knowledge and understanding. The art of questioning lies in knowing which questions to ask when. Address your first question to yourself: if you could press a magic button and get every piece of information you want, what would you want to know? The answer will immediately help you compose the right questions. If you are planning a meeting, prepare a list of any answers you need to obtain. As the meeting progresses, tick off the answers you receive. If new questions occur to you while others are talking, note them down and raise them later.

CHOOSING QUESTIONS

When preparing questions in advance, always look at the type of question that best meets your aims. You may want to initiate a discussion, obtain specific information, attain a particular end, or send a command cloaked as a query. However, be aware that prepared questions will rarely be enough – answers to them may be incomplete or may prompt a whole new line of questioning. Keep asking questions until you are satisfied that you have received the answers you require. When asking prepared questions, watch out for clues in the answers that you can follow up later with a new set of questions.

18 Write a list of questions before you start a meeting.

 19 Do not be afraid to pause while thinking of your next question.

CHOOSING QUESTIONS FOR DIFFERENT RESPONSES

TYPES OF QUESTION	EXAMPLES
OPEN Question does not invite any particular answer, but opens up discussion.	Q What do you think about the company setting up a canteen for all members of staff? A I think it is a good idea for a number of reasons.
CLOSED Question is specific and must be answered with a yes or a no, or with details as appropriate.	Q Do you ever read the company magazine or newsletter? A No.
FACT-FINDING Question is aimed at getting information on a particular subject.	Q What percentage of staff has replied to the employee attitude survey? A Out of 2,000 questionnaires we got 1,400 replies – that's 70 per cent.
FOLLOW-UP Question is intended to get more information or to elicit an opinion.	Q Is this a good response compared with last time? A Two-thirds is average, so this indicates reasonably good morale.
FEEDBACK Question is aimed at getting a particular type of information.	Q Do you think that communications within the company have improved? A Yes. I find it is useful being able to talk to my manager in our new fortnightly meetings.

STRIKING THE RIGHT TONE

Your tone of voice is a part of communication in itself – for example, you may convey anger by speaking harshly or sympathy by speaking softly. The wrong tone may generate a counter-productive response, so work on improving your ability to manage your tone of voice. Using a tape recorder, play back your voice. Is there any unintentional sharpness? Is it too conciliatory? Practise until you are happy with how you sound. You can often steer people towards agreement by using an optimistic and confident tone of voice.

20 Speak in as natural a tone as possible to create a warm environment.

READING EFFICIENTLY

The more you read and understand, the better informed you are. You can improve the speed and efficiency of your reading by using several easy techniques. Concentration is the key to all methods of reading faster and understanding more.

21 Use associations – especially striking ones – to enhance your memory.

READING EFFECTIVELY

The two most common methods used to read and fully understand a passage are to read it slowly, or to read it and then go back over it. Both methods are inefficient. Reading slowly has no effect on comprehension. The second method – known as regression – halves speed, but improves comprehension by only 3–7 per cent. Eliminate regression, and your reading speed will rise from the average of 250–300 words per minute (wpm) to 450–500 wpm with no loss of comprehension.

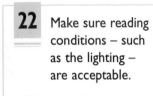

22 Make sure reading conditions – such as the lighting – are acceptable.

LEARNING TO SKIM-READ

Skim-reading can help you manage your time and reduce hours spent reading. In normal reading, the eyes make small, swift movements between groups of words (known as saccades), "fixing" briefly on each group. To read faster, you enlarge the groups and accelerate the move from one group to another. Before reading a book or proposal, if it has a contents, introduction, conclusion, and index, glance at these to decide what you need to read and what you do not.

A comfortable posture aids concentration

Book is flat on desk

IMPROVING YOUR SPEED ▶
When you are practising, read in bursts of about 20 minutes. Eliminate distractions when reading, and make sure that you are comfortable. Sit upright, in good lighting, with your book flat.

IMPROVING MEMORY

On average, it takes about seven hours to read a reasonably long book of about 100,000 words. You could halve this time with skim-reading. The object of learning how to read more quickly is to raise your maximum speed of reading by up to 80 per cent, without lowering your standard of comprehension. But reading and understanding at a faster rate do not help if you promptly forget what you have read, so you may need to improve your memory skills.

Memory is strongest after a few minutes, and 80 per cent is lost within 24 hours. An effective way to learn from books is to study for an hour, wait for a tenth of the time spent studying (6 minutes), review what you have studied, and then wait for 10 times the study period (in this instance, 10 hours) before you review again.

POINTS TO REMEMBER

- Powers of comprehension are usually overestimated.

- Lots of information can be picked up at a glance from illustrations and other visual material.

- Speed-reading can be learnt on a course or from books.

- Pages should be scanned down the centre, or diagonally, to achieve the most sense quickly.

- Time can be saved by looking at a book's contents, introductory pages, conclusion, and index, to check if it is worth reading.

- Memory can be improved by changing the way you learn and reviewing knowledge regularly.

TESTING YOUR COMPREHENSION

There are about 300 words on these pages under the headings "Reading Effectively", "Learning to Skim-Read", and "Improving Memory". To check how much you have taken in, read these again (it should take about a minute), then answer the questions below.

QUESTIONS:

1. What is regression?
2. What is the gain in comprehension from regression?
3. What is the average reading speed?
4. What is the objective of a fast-reading course?
5. What is the fast-reading speed range?

6. What is the main result of reading everything twice?
7. How much of your memory is lost within 24 hours?
8. What length is a reasonably long book?
9. How long should a reasonably long book take to skim-read?
10. When is memory strongest?

ANSWERS: 1. Going back over material again. 2. About 3–7 per cent. 3. 250–300 words per minute. 4. To raise maximum speed by up to 80 per cent without loss of comprehension. 5. 450–500 words per minute. 6. Reading everything twice merely halves your potential reading speed. 7. 80 per cent. 8. About 100,000 words. 9. About three-and-a-half hours. 10. After a few minutes.

TAKING NOTES

There is no need to rely on memory if you have mastered efficient methods of recording speech or condensing written communication. There are several different ways to make written records: experiment, and use whichever method suits you.

 23 Read your notes while what you have recorded is fresh in your mind.

TAKING LINEAR NOTES

If you are taking notes while people are speaking, do not try to write their words in longhand and in sequence or you will fail to keep up. Instead, listen to what is being said and note down the key points in your own words. Try writing a succinct explanation of each point, and use headings and numbers to structure your notes.

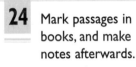 **24** Mark passages in books, and make notes afterwards.

USING SPEEDWRITING

There are classes for learning shorthand and speedwriting, but you can also teach yourself, and double your writing speed. In general, drop all vowels unless they begin a word, use numerals for numbers, and use standard abbreviations such as an ampersand (&) for "and". Use special abbreviations for common words or word parts, such as tt (that), th (the), t (to and it), r (are), s (is), v (very), f (of), g (-ing), and d (-ed).

◀ TAKING NOTES USING SPEEDWRITING

Space your notes in short paragraphs. Afterwards, read through quickly to check that everything makes sense to you.

Word is obvious from its context: this is "notes" not "nuts"

> *In th sm wy tht spdwrtg cn incrs th spd at whch y wrt nts wth a pn or pncl, y cn gtly incrs th spd at whch y mk nts usg a wrd pressr or typwrtr, if tht s hw y prfr t wrk.*
>
> *Whn y spdwrt, th shp f th wrds s unffctd by th dltd vwls, & y hv an entrly smpl & prctcl systm.*
>
> *Y my fnd tht evn whn y r sklld at spdwrtg, t s snsbl t spll unusual or dffclt wrds in fll. Als, f yr spdwrttn wrd cld b mstkn for 1 or 2 othr wrds, thn t s a gd pln t wrt th wrd in fll.*

Short words, like "at", can be written in full

Words are still easy to recognize when they are spelled without vowels

Words that are difficult to shorten or which may be hard to decipher are spelled out in full

USING MIND MAPS

Mind Maps®, which were devised by Tony Buzan, are a way of making visual notes. To make a Mind Map, write down a key word or phrase, or draw an image in the middle of a page. This is the subject of the Mind Map. As you make "notes", create "branches" from this central point. Each branch can have sub-branches (one idea leading to another), and different branches may link to each other. Use colour and images to illustrate points and to make the Mind Map easier to recall.

25 Use colour and illustrations to make your Mind Maps works of art.

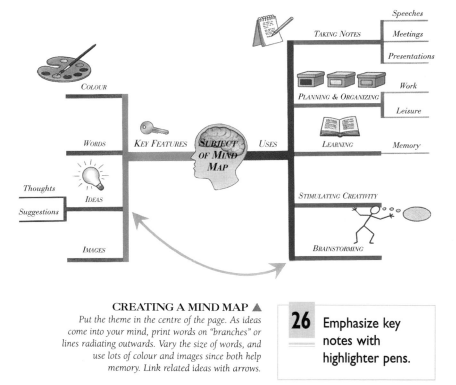

CREATING A MIND MAP ▲

Put the theme in the centre of the page. As ideas come into your mind, print words on "branches" or lines radiating outwards. Vary the size of words, and use lots of colour and images since both help memory. Link related ideas with arrows.

26 Emphasize key notes with highlighter pens.

EXCHANGING INFORMATION

Face-to-face, phone, or written communications can range from open warfare to perfect agreement. In every case, choose the right communication method to achieve your aim.

MAKING CONTACT

A satisfactory end to an encounter can never be guaranteed, but a good start is always possible. Your words and demeanour significantly affect the reactions of others, so use welcoming words to help start all proceedings on a positive note.

27 Stand up to greet or say goodbye to people – it is rude to stay seated.

POINTS TO REMEMBER

● Initial greetings should be as welcoming as possible.

● All attendees at a meeting need to be introduced to each other at the outset.

● Meetings are best ended courteously, even if they have involved disagreement.

● Behavioural and cultural differences (like whether it is customary to shake hands) should be respected at all times when travelling.

GREETING PEOPLE

The words used to greet people you know will be governed by the relationship. If the relationship is an equal one, you will almost certainly use first names and an informal salutation such as "Good morning", "How are you?", or "Nice to see you". With strangers, the greeting also acts as an introduction, so you announce your name ("I'm Mary Black") and follow up with an expression of polite pleasure ("It's good to meet you"). This implies friendly intent. Even if hostilities are possible, a civil verbal start is always wise.

USING BODILY CONTACT

If you are greeting a person with whom you are familiar, you may or may not shake hands, though it is more likely in a formal situation. In most situations, meet strangers with an extended hand, and offer a firm shake. Avoid offering a limp handshake, which may give an impression of weakness. Be aware of cultural rules that affect greetings between sexes. For example, it may be inappropriate for men and women to make any physical contact. Watch your posture, too: rise to your feet when receiving guests, and stand straight.

CULTURAL DIFFERENCES

In greetings, Spanish, French, Italian, and Latin American male colleagues may embrace each other. In contrast, the Japanese usually bow from a distance, perhaps shaking hands when better acquainted. They and the Chinese always accompany introductions with visiting cards.

Face each other and make eye contact

Use a two-arm goodbye to show more warmth than a handshake on its own

Stand up when saying goodbye

ENDING MEETINGS

When an agreement has been reached or a productive meeting is ending, make a point of emphasizing its success with your body language. If you are the host, remember to thank the other party or parties for their contribution and show them not just to the door of the meeting room but to the exit of the building. You may wish to say goodbye with a handshake, which will probably be warmer and more prolonged than when you greeted them. In other words, treat them as if they are your guests. The same analogy applies to the meeting's attendees – if they are on your territory, they should behave with courtesy. If the meeting has not been easy, remain courteous and civil, but without glossing over the failure.

◀ **SAYING A WARM GOODBYE**
Saying goodbye is likely to be a warmer experience than saying hello, especially if the encounter has been productive. In some countries, people are more likely to use physical contact, such as holding one of your arms when shaking hands.

PASSING ON INFORMATION

Managers spend much of their time delivering and receiving messages in person. This can be the most critical – and satisfying – arena of communication. Honesty and feedback are both essential if you are to achieve clarity and progress.

28 When giving positive feedback, state reasons for your praise.

FINDING INFORMATION

The workforce's need to obtain information and the ability of its managers to provide all types of information in the right way are crucial elements in any organization. Start by finding out which areas people most want to know about. Job security, working conditions, reward, location, and benefits are all important, and you should communicate any changes affecting these as soon and as directly as possible.

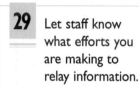

29 Let staff know what efforts you are making to relay information.

BEING UNDERSTOOD

Delivering a message that may be misunderstood is all too easy. It may happen because you are not clear about what you want to say; or because your language is vague even though your objectives are clear; or because your body language very subtly contradicts your verbal message. Another reason why it may happen is that you are communicating with someone who has decided in advance what the message is – without listening to you and regardless of what you are actually trying to say.

A useful way to avoid misinterpretation is to rehearse your message with an objective critic. Alternatively, get the recipients to repeat your message – you can then use their feedback to try to correct any misapprehensions. Use positive body language to emphasize your verbal message.

30 If in doubt about whether or not you should pass on information, do so.

GIVING FEEDBACK

Feedback is essential to communication – to check that you have understood the other person's message, and to react to what they have said and done. It can be difficult to give negative feedback, but remember that it is bad management to avoid doing this. When giving negative feedback, follow these simple rules to avoid any antagonism:

- Show an understanding of exactly what went wrong, and why;
- Draw out ways in which poor performance or behaviour can improve;
- Use questioning rather than assertions to let the staff member know what you think, and why;
- Aim to express your negative opinions honestly, but in a positive manner;
- Above all, take negative feedback away from the emotional zone by being objective, not personal.

31 Waste no time on people who refuse to understand you.

▼ HANDLING CONFLICT
Do not allow negative body language directed towards you to put you off. Sit up straight, make non-hostile eye contact, and give your message unambiguously.

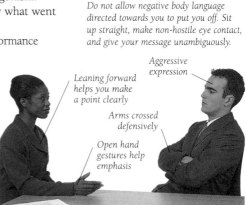

Aggressive expression

Leaning forward helps you make a point clearly

Arms crossed defensively

Open hand gestures help emphasis

REACTING HONESTLY

It is vital that you react honestly to the statements or actions of your employees. Give reasons for positive feedback, and use questions rather than assertions when giving negative feedback. Below are some examples that you can use:

❝ *I especially like how you backed up your argument with relevant facts, information on our competitors, and up-to-date statistics.* ❞

❝ *You are the right person for this job because…* ❞

❝ *Would you agree that this report is very unsatisfactory?* ❞

USING THE PHONE

Phones are very strong communication tools because they make people at a distance – and even total strangers – immediately accessible. Use the phone to create opportunities that otherwise would be much harder to exploit.

32 Keep a clock on your desk to monitor the time you spend on calls.

IMPROVING TECHNIQUE

Many people tend to take their phone skills for granted. However, phone skills can be improved by know-how and practice. Telesales people, who use the phone for "cold calls" to people they do not know, are experts. Basic telesales tips include:

33 Use features like "call waiting" to increase your effectiveness.

- Write down in advance what you want to cover and in what order;
- Speak slowly and pace yourself with the other person;
- Always be polite and friendly;
- Smile – a smiling face encourages a smiling voice and invites a positive response.

Smile – it raises your voice and makes it warm and friendly

Follow a script so that you do not lose track

Time your calls to make sure you do not overrun

◀ READING FROM A PREPARED SCRIPT

When making an important phone call, it is easy to be sidetracked. One way of avoiding this is to write a list of all the things you need to discuss and then tick them off as you go. Similarly, if you think a conversation might be difficult, write out useful phrases before phoning.

34 If you say you will return a call, make sure you do.

LEAVING MESSAGES

If you have answerphones and voice mail, deal with any incoming messages waiting for you as soon as you can, and always within 24 hours.

When leaving a message for someone else, start with your name, phone number, and the time of your call. Speak slowly and clearly, or your name, number, or both may be lost. When leaving an outgoing message, keep it brief and businesslike. If you can be specific about your time of return, or who should be contacted in your absence, change your outgoing message accordingly.

35 End answerphone messages by repeating your name and number.

MANAGING TELESALES

Telesales is a specialized form of communication. If you are involved with a telesales team, make sure the staff follow these golden rules:

● Work from a script;

● Do not pause or stop once you have started;

● Use "please" and "thank you" copiously;

● Put a mirror on the desk to check that you are smiling;

● Use "I" very sparingly.

GETTING THROUGH

You will not be able to communicate effectively if you fail to get through to the correct person. Do your research thoroughly to find the name of the person appropriate to your needs, and then, even if the person is a total stranger (and an important figure), adopt an intimate, confident approach when you phone them. For instance, when making the initial phone call, use the person's first name, and announce yourself by saying "This is so-and-so" (never "My name is so-and-so"). If the person in question is "in a meeting", ask when he or she will be free, and say when you will ring back. Then ring back later, and say your call is expected.

When you are through to the right person, never put down the phone without making your point – repeatedly, if possible. As with any verbal exchange, check that your message has been correctly understood by the other party.

36 Change your recorded phone message as and when your circumstances change.

USING INFORMATION TECHNOLOGY

New technology has greatly increased the choices for communicators. The personal computer, in both desktop and portable form, is a superb message centre for managers receiving and relaying information quickly all around the world.

37 Get expert advice on the best use of your information technology (IT).

USING THE FAX

Despite the advent of electronic mail (e-mail), facsimile (fax) is a useful form of communication that can help you manage your time. For example, if you have to pass on information to someone who wastes your time on the phone, using e-mail and fax will bypass this problem. The fax is extremely valuable for documents that need delivery and response faster than is possible by post.

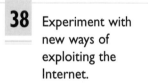

38 Experiment with new ways of exploiting the Internet.

USING E-MAIL

E-mail is fast, user-friendly, and versatile. It is a prime medium of communication within businesses, and accounts for more and more external messages. Keeping staff informed by e-mail also saves paper. However, e-mail can be abused, so follow these rules of "netiquette":

● Use meaningful subject titles;
● Be as brief as possible;
● Distinguish business mail from non-business;
● Be selective in the recipients of your e-mails;
● Avoid attaching extra files to your e-mail if you are mailing a lot of people at once;
● Never use obscene language and insults, and shun any racist or sexist mail.

POINTS TO REMEMBER

● Faxes can be either free-standing and paper-fed or linked to a personal computer.

● Managers without laptops or notebook computers can consider themselves under-equipped.

● The World Wide Web is the future of communications for most purposes.

● The Internet is a powerful communications tool mainly because of its ability to mix all media in real time.

● Cutting out communication waste helps everybody.

USING THE INTERNET

The Internet is transforming communication, as are internal networks, groupware, intranets (in-company internets), and the Extranet (which connects suppliers with customers). Use basic Web sites on the Internet to carry up-to-date information about your own organization for both customers and employees. Similarly, look at the Web sites of other companies for information on your competitors. The Internet is a valuable tool for all kinds of research, and for interactive dialogues. You can also use the Internet for buying and selling products.

▲ MAKING THE MOST OF TECHNOLOGY
Computers and information technology give staff immediate access to information of all kinds – from financial transactions to scientific data – throughout the world.

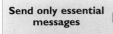

| Send only essential messages | → | Keep messages short | → | Avoid delays in replying |

CONTROLLING ▲
INFORMATION FLOW
To keep communication by electronic means fast and efficient, do not send irrelevant messages. Write succinctly and to the point, and reply to incoming messages as soon as possible.

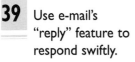

39 Use e-mail's "reply" feature to respond swiftly.

SPEEDING COMMUNICATION

The most effective way to improve the speed and quality of communication and information flow is to control the quantity. Whenever you send a message, ask yourself whether you really need to – if not, do not send it. Keep messages brief, because the shorter they are, the faster they can be processed. Check regular reports to see if anything can be shortened or eliminated – will anyone really notice if some regular communications are no longer made? Finally, do not procrastinate over responses: it is better, faster, and more efficient to answer immediately and keep your desk clear.

WRITING LETTERS

Documents that are written well, easy to understand, and keep to the point are composed by people who have clarified their thoughts before writing. Make your letters effective by thinking before you write, and always writing what you think.

 40 Visualize the reader when you are writing a letter or report.

41 Delegate writing routine replies to an assistant.

PRODUCING A PERFECT LETTER

Plan what you want to say in your letter

Write the whole letter without pause

Reread the letter when you have finished

Edit the letter by cutting ruthlessly

Check spelling and punctuation, then send

WRITING FOR RESULTS

All business letters have a purpose. The first rule of letter writing is to make that objective perfectly clear to your recipient. The second rule is to include all the information that the reader needs in order to understand your aim. Resist the temptation to write too much – try to fit your letter on one side of paper if you can. Ask a friendly critic to read any letters dealing with problematic situations.

COMPOSING CLEAR TEXT

The key to writing any business letter clearly and concisely is to keep your words simple and to the point. Use short words and sentences in preference to long, and active verbs rather than passive. Avoid double negatives, jargon, and archaic terminology (such as "notwithstanding" and "albeit"). Use natural, unforced diction: in other words, write as you talk, not as you think you should write. Do not revise until you have finished, and then cut fearlessly – editing always improves the impact of a letter.

 42 Avoid using complicated, unusual words or abstract terms – they may obscure your meaning.

STRUCTURING LETTERS

When structuring letters, apply the principles of direct mail. These are as follows:

- Attract the *attention* of the reader by stating why you are writing. Use humour if appropriate;
- Engage the reader's *interest* by arousing his or her curiosity about what you are saying;
- Provoke *desire* in the reader by making your proposal or product sound attractive;
- *Convince* the reader that your letter rings true by supplying references or guarantees;
- Stimulate *action* on the part of the reader by explaining what you expect him or her to do.

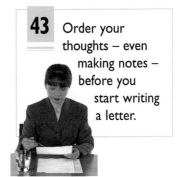

43 Order your thoughts – even making notes – before you start writing a letter.

◀ GETTING THE WRONG RESULT
This letter lacks clarity. It has not been thought through, it is badly spelled and punctuated, and unnecessarily wordy.

Dear Sir/Madam

I have heard on the grapevine that you are seeking a company which is capable of installing new computers for all your departments. I believe that my company can be safely appointed as one in which you might have complete confidence. Notwithstanding our somewhat limited experience in your industry, I have been advized by some one who used to work for you that we would be just right for the job. I am most enthousiastic, about the possibilities to mete you except please be advized that I will unfortunateley be unable to visit your office on Mondays, Tuesdays or on Friday afternoons. This is because at

Writer has not bothered to find out a contact

Meaning is unclear

Grammar and spelling are poor

Writer gives irrelevant details

Letter is on more than one page

GETTING THE ▶ RIGHT RESULT
This letter is clear, optimistic, and to the point. The writer has made an effort to be positive about the potential business relationship with the company.

Explains reason for letter

Has written letter on just one page

Today's date

Ms Martin
Planning Company
Street Name
Big Town

Knows to whom to send the letter

Dear Ms Martin

Further to our phone conversation last week, I have pleasure in enclosing a recent brochure.

You confirmed that your company is interested in installing new computer software, and I am sure we will be able to supply your needs.

Shows positive outlook

I look forward to hearing from you and to meeting you in the near future.

Yours sincerely

Suggests next step

Signature

ACQUIRING MORE SKILLS

The best communicators succeed in getting written
and verbal messages across to both individuals
and larger audiences, with understanding on all sides.

BRIEFING EFFECTIVELY

*Conveying to people the purpose, means,
and extent of a task entrusted to
them is a basic exercise in communication.
Learn how to brief effectively – whether
a client, colleague, or supplier – and you
will help a project on the way to success.*

44 Lean towards
giving too much
autonomy rather
than too little.

*Good eye
contact helps
retain
attention
as brief
is given*

▲ **GIVING PEOPLE INFORMATION**
*If you are providing a colleague or client with a written
brief, talk through this to expand or clarify any points
and to check that the brief is completely understood.*

SELECTING A BRIEF

There are a number of different types
of brief. Briefs may be about action to be
taken in the future, or they may be
de-briefing reports that explain what
has happened and why. If a client is
involved, the brief may be partly a
report and partly an action plan, in
which you give details of what you
propose, including what role the
client is to play. Get feedback from
the person you are briefing to check
you have given enough information.

45 Avoid over-briefing your staff, so they have a chance to use their initiative.

COMPILING A BRIEF

When briefing someone verbally, agree which of you will follow up with written confirmation of the brief. When compiling a briefing document:

- Put the aim at the top;
- Give the resources available;
- Provide a time horizon;
- Describe the method;
- If the brief is to produce a document, identify to whom this should be sent.

Even if you are delegating straightforward tasks, if you are specific, errors are less likely to be made.

▼ STRUCTURING A BRIEF

A written brief should be a clear document, setting out exactly what has to be done, when, and how. If relevant, state the budget allowance, plus the dates of any approval stages.

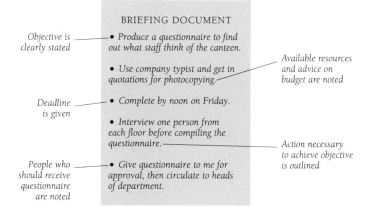

BRIEFING DOCUMENT

Objective is clearly stated — • *Produce a questionnaire to find out what staff think of the canteen.*

• *Use company typist and get in quotations for photocopying.* — *Available resources and advice on budget are noted*

Deadline is given — • *Complete by noon on Friday.*

• *Interview one person from each floor before compiling the questionnaire.* — *Action necessary to achieve objective is outlined*

People who should receive questionnaire are noted — • *Give questionnaire to me for approval, then circulate to heads of department.*

DELEGATING POWER

Most briefs involve delegation of power. If you are responsible for seeing that a task is completed and choose to nominate someone else to execute it, you are handing over power to that person and must outline their areas of responsibility in a brief. You should state how much you expect to be kept informed, and whether you will issue further instructions. If the project has a long timespan, remember to include the timing of reviews.

46 If you feel a project as briefed is not working out, do a re-brief fast.

COMMUNICATING ONE TO ONE

A meeting with a staff member can be formal (part of the way the unit is run) or informal (arranged to deal with a particular issue raised by either side). Use one-to-ones to check performance and find out if coaching or counselling is needed.

47 Ask all those invited to a meeting to come well prepared.

MEETING FORMALLY

There are no fixed guidelines for informal get-togethers, but for formal one-to-one meetings the rules are the same as for any other meeting. Get to the point quickly, stick to the agenda, sum up at the end, and make sure that the other side agrees with the summary. In any one-to-one meeting the relationship between a manager and subordinate has a tendency to move into one of dominance and submission. To make meetings productive, listen to the other person, aim for rational discussion, and be courteous. Remember, however, that a certain degree of confrontation may be perfectly healthy – and also unavoidable.

THINGS TO DO

1. Try to meet staff for formal one-to-one meetings at least monthly.

2. Stick to an agenda, and make sure you agree on any decisions.

3. Remember to listen to what is being said, and do not dominate the meeting.

BEING PREPARED

For regular meetings, preparation can make all the difference between a satisfactory or unsatisfactory outcome. Some companies stage one-to-ones between superiors and subordinates every two weeks to discuss any problems, define objectives, and deliver written performance reviews. For these one-to-ones, the managers distribute the reviews a few days beforehand. This preparation time gives the staff a chance to consider their response.

48 Remember that a "good meeting" is one that has produced results.

COACHING STAFF

Good managers must be good coaches who know how to encourage staff to raise their performance at work, improve their knowledge, and realize their full potential. Coaching is inherent in the whole management process and should not be confined simply to performance reviews and annual appraisals. As a manager, take the initiative by setting staff goals, by regularly encouraging staff to achieve higher standards, and by discussing any strengths or weaknesses. As the people being coached gain in confidence and performance, they will take on more responsibility for setting personal targets for improving at work.

49 Listen to your staff. Coaching or counselling may provide solutions to discontent.

COUNSELLING STAFF

Problems that arise either from work or from personal life can be helped by counselling. But unless you are a trained counsellor or have considerable experience, leave this to a professional, who will help people to confront and resolve their problems. If an employee has become unhappy over a situation, offer to arrange a counselling interview, and be sympathetic. The counsellor will try to help the individual get to the root of any problem. Give practical support when you can. If time off work will help, for example, make sure that it is available.

▼ **EXPLORING SOLUTIONS**
Before you suggest professional counselling to a member of staff, check that they agree they have a problem that needs help. Meet on neutral territory, where you will not be interrupted by people or phone calls.

50 Be aware of your staff's problems, because they affect performance.

CHAIRING MEETINGS SUCCESSFULLY

Most managers feel they spend too much time in meetings. However, a well-run meeting can be a productive way to communicate. When you are chairing a meeting, stay in control of the proceedings, and never let arguments get out of hand.

 51 Circulate all relevant papers before the start of a meeting.

 52 If a meeting is mainly for making decisions, ensure they are made.

PREPARING FOR A MEETING

When preparing for a meeting, ask yourself four key questions: What is the meeting for? Why is it being called? How will I know if it has been successful? Who should attend? These questions will determine whether the meeting is necessary. All meetings should have a purpose that will be achieved by their end. If final decisions are not made, there should at least be a plan of action. The most effective meetings are usually small with only vital people attending.

OPENING A MEETING

After making any necessary introductions, remind all those present of the meeting's purpose, what outcome it is expected to deliver, and when it will end. If there are ground rules, state them straight away. Check that everybody has any relevant papers and that the agenda is approved. If there has been a previous meeting, minutes may need approval and discussion, but do not discuss anything that already features on the agenda. Instead, go straight into the first item, preferably calling upon another participant to initiate the discussion.

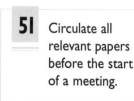 **53** If you are acting as chairperson, do not manipulate the meeting to your own advantage.

CONDUCTING A MEETING

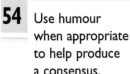

54 Use humour when appropriate to help produce a consensus.

Strike a balance between keeping the discussion process moving briskly forward and ensuring that everyone who wants to speak has a chance to state their opinion. The custom of debating an issue until a decision is made can be time-consuming and lead to tension. To prevent this, act as a timekeeper (make sure you have a watch or clock to hand). Set time limits to discussions so you can end the meeting at the appointed time.

CLOSING A MEETING

Allow yourself enough time for winding up a meeting. Summarize the discussion and check that others agree with your account; make decisions about unfinished business (which may include nominating someone to deal with it); and, finally, run through the implementation of any decisions taken, that is, the actions that will be the result of the meeting. Assign each action to a person, and attach a time target for completion.

55 Make sure you stick to the time limits for each item on an agenda.

COMMUNICATING BY SCREEN

Video conferences are not a substitute for face-to-face meetings but they may usefully complement them. They can be much more effective than a phone conference because participants like (and sometimes need) to see what is going on. Use video conferencing especially if you have far-flung offices that make regular meetings impractical.

◀ **USING VIDEO CONFERENCING**
Video conferencing, where everyone involved can see each other's body language and expressions while they talk, is a useful way of holding a meeting, and saves on travel time and costs.

REACHING AN AUDIENCE

*I*t pays to take care over preparing
and delivering speeches, whether for
presentations, seminars, conferences, or
training. Audiences find it easier to absorb
information by eye than by ear, so use
audio-visual (AV) techniques when possible.

 56 Finish your speech before the allotted time rather than long after it.

PREPARING SPEECHES

 57 Keep physical (or at least mental) back-ups in case your AV aids fail.

Give yourself enough time to compose and
rehearse your speech, including a final review. If
you write out the full text for a 30-minute
speech, you will need about 4,800 words, and the
writing will take many hours. Notes are obviously
quicker. Plan the 30 minutes around linked
themes. Summarize each theme, then add material
for each in note form. Allocate about 3 minutes per
theme if you are using AV aids (making 10 themes
in 30 minutes), otherwise 1–2 minutes for each.

MAKING YOUR POINT

Repetition, often a fault on the page, is essential
in oratory. Any speech is a performance. If you
plan to use notes, make them brief. By glancing at
a single word, you should be able to recall several
complex ideas. Refer to your notes, but do not
read straight from them. The brain's recall of
heard information is poor, so make your speech
as accessible as possible. Keep your language
clear, your sentences short, and preserve a smooth
flow, with a logical transition between points. The
last point you make should relate to the first.

 58 Ask questions of the audience if it is slow to ask questions of you.

▼ GETTING THROUGH
*The three crucial steps in getting your
message across are to tell the audience
what you are going to say, say it, and
then repeat what you have said.*

| Introduce the message | → | Convey the message | → | Repeat the message |

59 Speak for 20–45 minutes maximum – this is the length of the average person's attention span.

ENCOURAGING REACTION

If you can, speak without any notes and move confidently around the stage. This removes the psychological barrier of the podium and makes you and your speech more accessible. As you speak, focus on the centre of the audience, about two-thirds of the way back. People listening will usually be inclined to feel positive towards you rather than hostile, so allow their support to give you confidence. Make eye contact, and encourage the audience to participate – asking people questions, either en masse or individually, works well. Making them laugh also breaks the ice.

USING VISUAL AIDS

The most commonly used visual media are probably still the 35-mm slide projector and the overhead projector. For smaller audiences, the flip-chart and writing board are effective. The most powerful AV media use colour and images, including moving ones. Technology has made this easy, fast, and cheap, linking PCs to projectors. Whatever you use, make sure that the technical operation is foolproof and that the visual material is the best possible. If appropriate, support your speech by giving the audience copies of notes and visual materials.

▼ **PRESENTING SUCCESSFULLY**
Make your body language positive. Use gestures to reinforce your points – but sparingly. If you are fluent and confident without notes, do not use them.

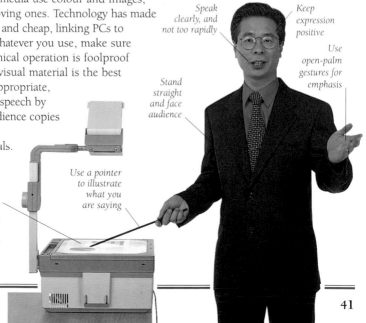

Speak clearly, and not too rapidly

Keep expression positive

Use open-palm gestures for emphasis

Stand straight and face audience

Use a pointer to illustrate what you are saying

Check that material on overhead projector is ready in order

TRAINING FOR RESULTS

Leading a training session for staff is a vital form of communication. Speak to trainees as you would to any audience: be confident, make eye contact, and invite questions. Training courses are often most effective when they are intensive and are held over a few days away from the office. By talking to staff in informal discussion groups or in conversation outside training sessions, you will also be able to get valuable feedback on all aspects of the organization. Feedback on the training itself is vital to check that the process is worthwhile.

60 If possible, invite a famous speaker to a seminar or conference.

61 Check regularly that your staff are getting the training they require.

HOLDING A SEMINAR

Internal seminars and workshops provide training in areas that are important to an organization. They are working events, practical, informal, and focused on specific aims. If you are running an internal event, invite only relevant personnel; it is often valuable for senior management to attend. Use external seminars to introduce changes to customers and suppliers, or to provide a selling opportunity. Invite top management to contribute to these seminars with an introductory or concluding speech, or a non-selling lecture.

SPEAKING AT A SEMINAR

If you are speaking at either an internal or external seminar, ask the organizer what subjects other speakers will be covering to make sure you do not repeat each other. Check how long you will be expected to talk, and whether there will be a question-and-answer session afterwards. If you are speaking without a microphone, make sure the audience can hear you at the back of the room (ask them, if necessary). Do not talk too quickly, and keep an eye on a watch or clock to ensure that you speak only for the allotted time.

62 Ask other managers if they would like to speak at seminars.

PLANNING A CONFERENCE

Conferences are more formal and larger than seminars. In the same way that meetings must have a purpose, all conferences should have objectives. These will be the basis of any agenda, and will provide a springboard for discussions. Internal sales conferences, in particular, are usually motivational events. Like all conferences, they require first-class venues, professional presenters, excellent sets and audio-visuals, and careful planning. Well in advance, decide who will address the conference. If you can arrange for a guest speaker to liven up the proceedings, it will help maintain the audience's interest and enthusiasm. Make sure that all speakers know when they are expected to make their speech and for how long they are scheduled to talk.

POINTS TO REMEMBER

- The more planning and thought that go into an event, the more it is likely to achieve.
- Any message will usually be reinforced if accompanied by good audio-visual technology.
- Staff at seminars or conferences should be treated with as much respect and care as suppliers.
- Showbusiness or professional speakers can be hired (at a price) to talk at company events.
- Conferences and seminars always need to be followed up, or they may be of little benefit.

63 Get some recommendations if selecting a new conference venue.

CHOOSING A VENUE

The venue is part of the message, and speaks volumes to those who are attending. When you are deciding where to hold a conference or seminar, think carefully about what is required, and always choose a venue that is suitable for the scale and type of event. For a large conference, you need a space that easily accommodates everyone. However, for a workshop, you may only need one medium-sized room plus a few smaller ones, where trainees can work together in groups or teams. Before booking a venue, check that everything you require will be available, such as electronic and other equipment (like microphones and projectors), comfortable seating for all attendees, and catering.

DO'S AND DON'TS

- ✔ Do check attendees know how to get to the venue and have means of transport.
- ✔ Do plan a schedule of events, including refreshment breaks.
- ✔ Do be ready to adapt the agenda in case proceedings overrun.

- ✘ Don't expect people to make impromptu, unprepared speeches at a conference.
- ✘ Don't invite people to seminars if their presence is not vital.
- ✘ Don't forget to obtain feedback to check on an event's success.

COMMUNICATING TO SELL

Selling is basic to business, and not only in persuading external customers to buy. In all business situations, you can use established sales techniques to gain the agreement of others, enlist support, obtain resources, and overcome any opposition.

 64 If you want to "soft sell", make your point in the form of a question.

Non-threatening smile

Open-palm gesture

SOFT SELLING

All good selling is "soft": you seek to establish a need and promise to fulfil that need. You can use this approach at work, and adapt your "sales pitch" to suit the situation. Techniques include:
● Exploring a situation by using questions and listening, rather than making statements;
● Letting others reply, even at the price of pauses;
● Showing sympathetic understanding if you encounter resistance – but persevering until the other person accepts your view.

◀ **USING SOFT-SELLING TECHNIQUES**
Smiling and using upturned hands with open palms are soft-selling techniques. Both are friendly, persuasive, and non-threatening. The hand gesture also adds emphasis.

HARD SELLING

The old-fashioned hard-sell method works by putting people on the spot and forcing them to make a decision. If you are trying to implement an idea at work, be positive and use hard selling when you get close to a deal. Hard-sell tactics include:
● Making a "final, final" offer;
● Stressing loss of opportunity;
● Emphasizing a competititve situation;
● Making a hard, clear proposition;
● Pressing for immediate agreement.

65 Listen to objections from potential customers – they may give clues to help you make the sale.

SELLING BY WRITTEN WORD

Using written documents to sell – whether you are trying to sell a product by mail or are "selling" a proposal to colleagues – follows some apparently paradoxical rules. For instance, in direct marketing to outsiders, long letters markedly outsell short ones. However, when sending internal memos, short documents are more effective. Long or short, explain at the beginning of the document why you are writing. Gain the readers' interest, keep to the point, make your case convincing, and end with a concise, clear and positive summary.

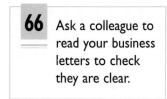

66 Ask a colleague to read your business letters to check they are clear.

UTILIZING COMPUTERS

The personal computer has evolved as a powerful sales aid. For example, you can store the names and addresses of potential customers on a database, and even call up files relating to a client while you are talking to them on the phone. Having facts on screen can make you more efficient and help you close a deal. Computers are particularly useful for selling financial services: when details of a buyer's finances are input, many programs will generate personalized proposals.

67 Approach any sale as a joint exercise between you and the buyer.

SELLING IDEAS AND CONCEPTS

Basic sales techniques are applicable to many essential management tasks. Mastering "the patter" can be crucial to success inside your organization, as well as outside. Try some of the soft- and hard-sell phrases below next time you want to sell an idea.

❝ *I developed this from something you said to me the other day.* ❞

❝ *This is what you've been looking for. If we don't do it, one of our competitors will for sure.* ❞

❝ *We haven't got long to consider this latest proposal – it's basically now or never.* ❞

❝ *Nobody else could do this as well as we could.* ❞

NEGOTIATING TO WIN

*A*ll negotiation requires first-class communication skills. You need to be able to put forward proposals clearly and to understand exactly what the other side is offering. Such skills are vital in all kinds of management, so try to improve them.

 68 Choose naturally differing personality types in your negotiating team.

STAGES OF NEGOTIATION

Plan your strategy and tactics

Put forward your proposal

State your position and begin debating

Bargain with the other side

Sum up and ratify agreement

PREPARING FOR TALKS

The better prepared a negotiation, the greater its chances of success. Start by deciding on your objectives. Next, decide who will conduct the negotiation. Will it be one person or a team? If it is a team, who will form the best partnerships? Ensure the team thoroughly researches the issues and their positions. The research will help to determine the agenda agreed with the other side. Have the team do at least one role-play beforehand. Finally, develop your minimum position – that is, the least you will settle for.

MASTERING TECHNIQUES

Negotiating experts usually base their approach around needs – generally the needs of the other side. When you enter negotiations "working for the other side's needs", you are taking maximum control with minimum risk. Good timing is crucial. During the debating and bargaining stages, you need to judge what the other side is thinking and pick your moment to raise or alter your offer, reject a proposal, or introduce a new element. Always try to shift the opposition from an adversarial stance towards an alliance. Asking leading questions, such as "Are you ready to sign?", is one way to soften your stance while gaining attention, getting and giving information, and stimulating thought.

NEGOTIATING TO BUY

Two things are essential when you are negotiating to buy. Firstly, decide exactly what you need (not what you want). Remember that the seller's job is to persuade you that your needs and their offer are one and the same. Secondly, decide how much you are prepared to pay. Set yourself an upper limit, and do not exceed it. In such a negotiation, the first person to name a price is at a disadvantage, so try to persuade the other side to be the first to make a financial offer.

69 Think about your ideal outcome – and how you can achieve it.

70 Share helpful information with suppliers – long term, it may help you win a better deal.

WORKING WITH SUPPLIERS

The traditional way to negotiate with suppliers is to get a number of quotes in from more than one supplier (to create healthy competition), listen to the quotes, bargain hard, ask for substantial cuts, raise your offer a little, and settle for the lowest possible price. If the supplier fails on quality or delivery, you negotiate again.

A newer, better approach is to choose the best suppliers, and negotiate in a way that achieves lower costs and shared profits for both sides. With this approach, instead of making price the only issue, you first negotiate reliability and other non-price issues before discussing actual costs.

BARGAINING WITH STAFF

One-to-one meetings can be useful for individual negotiations with staff on issues like quality of work and productivity. When you conclude an agreement, remember that it helps if the other side thinks that they have won something, even if they have not. If you ever have to deal with hostile professional negotiators (perhaps when a union is involved), and if their demands are above your maximum position, keep calm and concentrate on securing a result within your limits.

71 Remember that people seldom go on strike over non-pay issues.

COMPILING REPORTS

Reports are formal documents that will be read by others. They must always be accurate and well laid out, finishing with a definite conclusion. If you have been asked to write a report, make sure that it fulfils all the requirements of your original brief.

 72 Be ruthless: cut out all unnecessary words in your report.

RESEARCHING A REPORT

If you are reporting on an activity of your own, check every fact to ensure accuracy. If you have been asked to report on a subject – say, a new market for a product – write down what you need to know as a series of points. Then note the sources you can tap and match them to the points, making sure everything is covered. Before finalizing, get information supplied by one source confirmed by at least one other reliable authority.

 **73** Tailor reports to suit what you know about the recipients.

DO'S & DONT'S

✔ Do make each report interesting.

✔ Do use verbatim quotes from interviewees.

✔ Do emphasize your most important findings and facts.

✔ Do use numbered paragraphs to make cross-referencing easier and to keep points separate.

✔ Do use headings for changes of subject and subheadings for related themes.

✘ Don't waffle or write unbroken, long paragraphs.

✘ Don't overuse the first person singular ("I") or allow your personal prejudices to show.

✘ Don't indulge in digressions or go off at tangents.

✘ Don't draw conclusions from insufficient evidence.

✘ Don't print your report without thoroughly checking your sources.

STRUCTURING A REPORT

Write the purpose of a report and summarize its main conclusions in your opening paragraphs. In the body of the report, support your findings with evidence, set down in a logical sequence, in numbered paragraphs. Use headings, sub-headings, and bullet points, all of which are effective structural aids, drawing attention to key facts. Use underlining and bold type for emphasis. End the report with recommendations for action in summary form.

ENSURING CLARITY

Reports are not works of literature, but good ones follow the rules of good writing. Avoid ambiguities. If you are unsure about your conclusions, state the alternatives and invite the readers to make up their own minds. Express yourself in short sentences. Above all, put yourself in the readers' shoes. Will they understand what you mean? If you can, get a friend or colleague to read the report before you distribute it.

74 Seize opportunities to present your report in person to an audience.

75 Avoid making any unsupported assertions or conclusions.

BEING CONCISE

If you are concise, you will reinforce the clarity of your report. Never use two words where one will do, or three where two are enough. Use short words rather than long ones. Spend time on the report's main conclusion, and place smaller summaries at the start of each section. When reading through the report, cut where you can. This should improve the sense of the text.

PRESENTING A REPORT

If you are going to make a verbal presentation of your report, ask yourself what matters more: deliberation or impact? If you are putting a case forward at a meeting, you should distribute your report then, and give a summary using AV aids if possible. Where your position is more neutral – with a feasibility study, perhaps – distribute the report in advance. Then make sure you come to the meeting well prepared for likely questions and objections.

▲ **PRESENTING USING AV AIDS**
Presenting your conclusions with excellent AV aids and speaking skills increases the impact of a report handed out at a meeting. Visual messages sell a report in an immediate way.

WRITING PROPOSALS

A proposal differs from a report in that it is a selling document, which should persuade readers to commit to whatever you are proposing. You could use an internal proposal, for example, to argue for extra company investment in computers or staff.

 76 Enlist allies in preparing and lobbying for your proposal.

DRAFTING A PROPOSAL

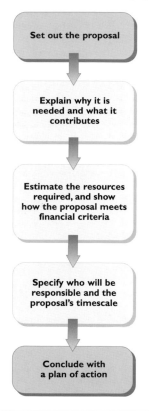

Set out the proposal

Explain why it is needed and what it contributes

Estimate the resources required, and show how the proposal meets financial criteria

Specify who will be responsible and the proposal's timescale

Conclude with a plan of action

RESEARCHING A PROPOSAL

To be successful, projects must be consistent with the overall aims of an organization. Before you write a proposal, research whether and how it fits into the wider scheme of the organization. When planning your research:

- Find out how the proposal would fit company strategy, and if there are any conflicting relevant activities that are either under way or planned for the future;
- Find out which aspects (such as finances, human resources, and legal implications) must be taken into account, and what repercussions these might possibly have for the organization;
- Ask those in a position to make decisions what objectives they would like to achieve in the form of short-term, medium-term, and long-term results;
- Gather together all necessary information to support the proposal, in readiness to go on to the next stage: planning.

 77 Ask yourself honestly why one proposal might fail and another might succeed.

PLANNING A PROPOSAL

Structure a proposal following the same basic format as a report. State the proposal in a summary at the beginning; use headings as you develop your argument; then repeat your main points in a conclusion at the end. Make your approach upbeat – your enthusiasm should convince others of your ability to deliver the proposed outcome. If any risk is involved, explain that you have already fully considered potential drawbacks, and concentrate on positive benefits.

78 Use soft-sell techniques to get your proposal accepted.

QUESTIONS TO ASK YOURSELF

Q How much will the proposal cost, and who will be involved?

Q What will be the benefits – economic, marketing, quality – if the proposal is accepted?

Q How will the proposal be implemented?

Q Why is it being put forward at this time?

Q Why do you believe the proposed plan will succeed?

FOLLOWING UP

When you distribute a proposal, make sure that the recipients know when and how you plan to follow it up, or whether you expect a written response. Whether the proposal is to colleagues within your company, or to an outside supplier or customer, it is useful to follow up with a meeting where the proposal can be discussed. If possible, make a presentation at the meeting using AV aids, since the more visual impact a proposal has, the greater its chances of success. Remember, though, that no matter how strong the presentation, it will not sell a definitely weak proposal.

WRITING AN EFFECTIVE BUSINESS PLAN

If you require funding in order to set up a business, potential finance lenders will want to see a business plan. Write this document with a clear proposal, discussion, and conclusion. Support your proposal with detailed facts and figures projected over a relevant period (usually at least three years). The business plan must show that you have a good grasp of financial matters, that you have considered all factors, making best and worst case assumptions, and that there is a good chance of profit if the plan goes ahead.

CREATING PLANS
Make sure your business plan looks professional. Include title and contents pages, and bind the plan securely between covers.

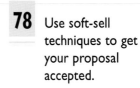

MAKING A VISUAL IMPACT

Even the most promising proposal or report can suffer from poor layout, graphics, or typography. Similarly, a brilliantly designed document carries greater – perhaps decisive – impact. If practical, use professionals for this kind of work.

 79 Add meaningful headlines and captions – people read them first.

 80 Use colour images, graphs, and charts in documents when possible.

ASSESSING DESIGN NEEDS

Whatever the document, aim for the highest practicable design standards, but vary the approach to meet the need. For example, the design of external sales documents must complement your corporate image and "advertise" the organization, using its logo properly and projecting high quality. Internal documents have more freedom. Unless you have been trained in design, you may need to employ a professional designer to give documents extra visual impact. Choose someone experienced who specializes in this type of work.

USING A DESIGNER

If you decide to employ a professional designer, how do you find someone whose work fits the style you are looking for? Always look at a designer's portfolio since their previous work is a good indication of what they can do. Give the designer a clear brief at the outset. Explain fully what you want designed, ask for roughs if appropriate, and give dates for any review stages and deadlines. Do not be afraid to reject preliminary work and re-brief to ensure that ultimately you get what you want. Remember that your judgment should not just be based on whether or not you "like" the design, but rather on whether it meets the business aims.

81 Keep an eye on design work as it progresses so you can head off errors or re-brief early.

DESIGNING FOR CLARITY

One of the most important design decisions is the choice of font (typeface). Modern software programmes offer a fantastic range, but the main font must be clear and highly readable. If your budget allows the use of colour, by all means make the most of it. However, avoid printing words over colour or illustrations, since this may affect legibility. White type on a black background is also hard to read. Resist gimmicks: keep the design simple and suited to its purpose.

POINTS TO REMEMBER

● Using many different fonts at the same time can lead to a confusing overall look.

● Legibility is very important – the type should not be too small.

● A well-designed document is one that you enjoy looking at, but that also serves its function.

Type layout is very unprofessional

Coloured paper is a bad choice

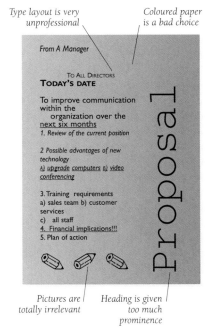

Pictures are totally irrelevant

Heading is given too much prominence

Aligned type is easy to read

Aim of proposal is in clear bold type

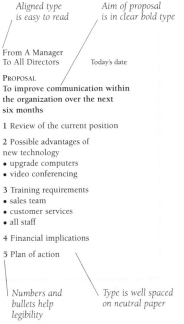

Numbers and bullets help legibility

Type is well spaced on neutral paper

▲ **GETTING IT WRONG**
This document looks messy for a number of reasons: it uses too many type styles inconsistently, has uneven spacing and unnecessary illustrations. Its appearance suggests it was written in a hurry.

▲ **GETTING IT RIGHT**
Using bold numbers and bullets for different subjects, aligning the type, and spacing the items consistently make the first page of this proposal look professional. It sends a positive message.

COMMUNICATING FOR RESULTS

The challenge to managers today lies in knowing how to exploit different types of media and use them to influence the public most effectively.

CREATING AN IDENTITY

A corporate identity is what enables an organization to be easily recognized by the public and within industry, and helps to establish its position in the market. If your budget allows, enlist the services of a designer or consultant to create an identity.

82 Get the opinion of trusted outsiders before finalizing a new logo.

83 Keep vision and mission statements short and action-oriented.

CONSIDERING IMAGE

The type of corporate identity you choose influences the way your organization is perceived. The right image will strongly influence audience perceptions in your favour. Similarly, the wrong image gives an undesirable message to employees and the public. Ideally, a corporate identity should make a visual impact – perhaps including a striking logo or the use of colours – since this is a key element of effective communication. Before you brief anyone to design a new identity, decide what image you wish to convey, and check that you have your colleagues' support and agreement.

CHANGING AN IDENTITY

Every organization has an identity – meaning how it is perceived by others – but many leave that identity to chance. However, if you do this you are neglecting a powerful marketing and recruitment tool. To create an effective corporate identity, you should decide on a central purpose and strategy (a "vision" and "mission"), as well as the image that you want to convey. Compare that desired image with current perceptions and act to close the gap.

84 Check large corporate Web sites to see what others are doing.

USING AN IDENTITY

Having settled on an identity, aim to use every piece of design, from the organization's reports to letterheads, from interiors to logos, to deliver a coherent message. You can also stamp an identity on internal documents, like memos, to emphasize the organization's image. Ensure that the identity is consistent in all of your communication media. Monitor the ways in which the identity is used. Occasionally, you may need to revise this use, to ensure that perceptions match your strategic need.

▼ USING LOGOS ON PRODUCTS

Coca-Cola's distinctive logo and the use of red and white on its packaging make the product instantly recognizable. This strong identity helped to make Coca-Cola a market leader worldwide.

Plastic bottle echoes shape of glass bottle

Traditional glass bottle distinguishes Coca-Cola from other cola drinks

Bright red cans carry logo

USING WEB SITES

The World Wide Web is a major source of corporate information, and often provides product and service news as well. Anybody can develop a site, but it is valuable to remember the following points:

● Professionals will always make a better job of developing a Web site. Ask them to cut down the preliminaries (the welcoming pages of your site) to the minimum: wading through page after page is irritating, time-wasting, and off-putting to site visitors.

● If you come across an effective site, do not hesitate to copy the elements that make it work, or adapt them to suit your organization.

● Watch out for bad habits, such as over-using graphics. This slows down access.

LLYFRGELL COLEG MENAI LIBRARY 55

USING PUBLIC RELATIONS

All managers have to consider the public impact of their actions. Public relations (PR) is the term used to describe the way issues and messages are communicated between an organization and the public. Handle PR internally, or employ experts.

 85 Get your PR people to handle potentially difficult media situations.

 **86** If you meet a hostile journalist, keep your cool; say nothing that could damage good PR.

RAISING YOUR PROFILE

An organization's reputation is one of its most critical assets. The role of public relations is to build and enhance a good reputation, and to prevent or mitigate damage to that reputation. Expert PR practitioners work to a plan that is linked to the organization's overall long-term strategy. They will use a number of techniques to supplement paid advertising campaigns and increase public awareness. The most effective advertising is favourable word-of-mouth: this free promotion should be one of PR's main objectives.

WORKING WITH PR

In small companies, PR may be handled by management or by employees who are not necessarily specialists in dealing with press or publicity. In larger organizations, internal PR departments are indispensable, mainly for the routine tasks of keeping in touch with and responding to the media and interest groups. If you have a PR department or employ a PR company, make sure that the relevant people are informed about things likely to generate public interest – from new products to the latest company results.

87 If bad news breaks, admit the reality to everyone – especially yourself.

EMPLOYING CONSULTANTS

▼ BRIEFING CONSULTANTS
When you initially employ a PR company, introduce the PR consultants to the relevant personnel in your organization. Explain the brief and check that the consultants know whom to contact in future if the need arises.

Generally, if you have a new message to relay to the public, it makes sense to use specialist PR consultants. Even large corporations with dedicated internal departments are likely to employ consultants occasionally. These range from multinational empires to one-person bands. They should be expert in everything from crisis management to arranging conferences, from launching products to introducing a new manager. Their contacts are usually extensive, and they should be capable of original ideas as well as effective execution. Always look at past work and take up references. Remember, too, that however able the PR company, it can only be as good as its client, and relies heavily on the brief.

USING PR EFFECTIVELY

The main thing to remember in using PR is that the quantity of coverage is less important than quality. PR is naturally cheaper than advertising, but you get what you pay for, so set aside a reasonable budget. Also, remember that publicity is double-edged and unpredictable, and PR officers are not to be blamed automatically if the media take a hostile turn. Nor can PR officers compensate for the lack of a proper brief. You need them to work with you to devise a PR strategy, but as in any supplier relationship, you must outline their duties and your expectations clearly. Agree on a plan of action, and review progress of the campaign at regular intervals.

POINTS TO REMEMBER

● PR departments and consultants must be kept informed about the organization's public actions.

● Staff should be trained and told when to speak to the media, and how to deal with enquiries.

● PR consultants need to be properly briefed so that they know what is expected of them.

● PR can be used as a valuable complement to advertising.

● Using PR to project the image of an organization can improve overall public perceptions.

USING PRINT MEDIA

Published articles that mention your organization or products can be more credible to the public than straightforward advertising. Take advantage of opportunities for you or your PR consultant to get features and news stories into print, at both national and local level. Editors are usually hungry for copy, so do not be shy about making a direct approach to them. Some editors can be extremely demanding, so check that you know exactly what the paper or magazine wants, and hire professional help if necessary. In the same way, ensure that your press releases are clear and well written.

88 Buy and read the newspapers and magazines you want to influence.

POINTS TO REMEMBER

● News releases should be tailored to the needs of the press.

● Your company will benefit if you find time for media people.

● It is always safer to stick to the truth – the facts are sure to be uncovered eventually.

● The more accessible you are to the media, the more coverage you will be given.

USING RADIO

The numerous radio programmes at local and national level can be a valuable asset to any publicity campaign. Radio provides companies with an alternative, immediate way to reach large target audiences. Before agreeing to take part in a programme, check on the size and type of audience it will reach. You do not want to find yourself talking only to a few night-owls. Talk to radio personalities on equal terms, and give honest answers. Try to control the interview so that you talk the most and can get your message across.

USING TELEVISION

Television is an extremely powerful and seductive medium, so accept any invitations to appear on TV, so long as you are confident in front of a camera. Get training in how to handle an interview beforehand. The technique is to look and be natural, and to answer questions as you would away from the camera. Managers can get valuable practice for appearing on real TV by taking part in video conferences, especially if they are exposed to unexpected questions.

89 Treat cameras and microphones as if they were friendly people.

TALKING TO JOURNALISTS

It always pays to cultivate good relations with the press and journalists who work in radio and TV. However, remember that journalists are not interested in serving your ends, but in getting a good story – preferably one that beats their competitors. Play fair: giving exclusives to one journalist will irritate the others – and you do not want journalists as enemies. If journalists contact you for your comment on something, and you are not confident about what you should say, ask if you can phone them back with a statement.

90 If you have a good relationship with the press, exploit it to the full.

▼ **CONVEYING THE RIGHT MESSAGE**
When talking to journalists, think before you make a response; give straightforward answers, and speak with confidence.

Eye contact shows lack of anything to hide

Journalist takes occasional notes to support taped conversation

Open body language conveys willingness to be helpful

Taping interview ensures you should be quoted accurately

USING STATISTICS

Readers, TV viewers, and radio listeners are always impressed by statistics, even when they cannot check their relevance or accuracy. Indeed, the more statistics you can muster in support of an argument, whether in a newspaper article or during an interview for broadcasting, the more convincing it will appear to an audience.

One feature of statistics is that the same data can be presented in a favourable or unfavourable light, depending on how you handle the figures. For example, if statistics show an increase of, say, 258 per cent, this may not be as good as it sounds. If the previous period was barely profitable, you may still really be showing poor results.

ADVERTISING EFFECTIVELY

The creative ideas and designs of good advertisements (which can be in any medium) must always be linked to a clear, measurable selling purpose. Ensure that your advertising gives potential customers a good reason to buy your product or services.

91 Make sure your product matches the promise, or advertising will fail.

92 Target your advertising for maximum impact.

93 Be as creative as possible – you can succeed on a small budget.

PLANNING ADVERTISING

Whether you are embarking on an expensive long-term campaign or placing a single advertisement on the recruitment pages of a newspaper, plan your advertising carefully. All advertisements convey a public message about your organization. What you are advertising and the size of your budget will influence the media you choose. Will you use TV, radio, newspapers, magazines, posters, hoardings, the Internet, or direct mail, for instance? If you use more than one, the messages in different media should reinforce each other. For a big campaign, you should employ a specialized advertising agency.

USING A ▶ TARGET GROUP

In this case study, the campaign was successful because the agency knew its target group well. It realized that it was not the quantity of advertising that would affect the target group most, but the quality of the publication in which the advertising was found.

CASE STUDY
A shoe company wanted to launch a brand of distinctive, fashion boots. The company employed an advertising agency, whose customer research showed that the market for such boots was limited. The agency felt that the brand could not support a heavy advertising campaign aimed at everyone who might buy the boots. Instead it decided to target its efforts at a smaller group of what it termed "style-leaders".

The desire to buy would trickle down from this select group to other purchasers. The agency placed advertisements in a trend-setting magazine to attract the style-leaders, even though research showed the magazine was read by few potential purchasers.

The strategy worked: the style-leaders bought the boots followed by thousands of buyers who had never seen the advertisement. Sales multiplied more than fivefold.

MEASURING AWARENESS

Researching the market is crucial, because the information provides a yardstick for judging whether advertising is working. If necessary employ market research specialists to provide valuable feedback. For example, a survey can reveal the extent of public awareness about an advertised product before, during, and after a campaign. If appropriate, adapt any follow-up advertising to reach a new target audience.

94 Use panels of consumers to test advertisements before release.

USING THE INTERNET

An increasing number of organizations are successfully advertising on the World Wide Web. One big computer company achieves 10 per cent of its sales from its 24-hour, 7-days-a-week Web "store". There are various reasons why advertising on the Internet is so popular:

● You can advertise products and direct-sell simultaneously;

● Images can move, which adds to effectiveness;

● Costs are quite low compared with other media;

● The Web is potentially the largest single medium for advertising many goods and services, in industrial products, as well as in consumer areas.

▲ COMPANY WEB SITES
Use your site on the World Wide Web to sell products, advertise, and provide information. You may take spots on other people's sites, even if you have your own.

USING DIRECT MAIL

The beauty of a direct mail campaign – when you try to sell your product or services to selected customers by post – is that the marketing message goes straight to a target group. This means that the response and cost-effectiveness of your direct mailing can be accurately measured. For maximum effectiveness, you must have the right list for mailing – compiled by your own staff or bought from a mailing-list company Add the right offer, and a direct mailshot should work well. Research shows you are more likely to get a response if there are a number of items in the envelope. If your target group is small, you may be able to handle your mailings without the need for a dedicated department or direct mail specialists.

COMMUNICATING AT WORK

The techniques used for external communications can also be used effectively inside an organization, though on a much smaller scale and budget. Exploit these methods to ensure that messages reach your staff with real impact.

95 Attend social events at work to get informal staff feedback.

96 Get professional advice on media techniques you can use internally.

WINNING OVER EMPLOYEES

Employees are people who depend vitally on their management's services for their livelihoods. They are, in fact, an organization's most important "customers". Similarly, each department inside an organization is a "customer" of another; they all depend on each other to provide their services effectively. All lines of communication should be open between departments.

Good employers take every opportunity and use every transaction with employees to show that they really believe that people are valuable assets. Communication is important to get this message across. Target employees for offers tailored to their needs: for example, further education, community projects, and sports facilities.

MARKETING FROM INSIDE

In-company marketing can operate as efficiently as external marketing in catching the attention of people, engaging their interest, arousing their wish to participate, convincing them to follow your lead, and encouraging the behaviour you want. Various devices – from competitions to "consumer" panels – can all be used effectively to put across the management message in direct and powerful terms. Remember not to talk down to the audience, and always tell the truth.

97 Use logos on all stationery to promote company awareness.

USING DIFFERENT MEDIA INSIDE AN ORGANIZATION

TYPE OF MEDIUM	FACTORS TO CONSIDER
HANDOUTS Including questionnaires, notices, and memos.	• These are useful to explain and report issues affecting employees, for example, results of attitude surveys. • Even if kept as brief and concise as possible, handouts create an unavoidable build-up of paper, and are frequently consigned to the waste-bin unread.
MEETINGS AND SOCIAL EVENTS Including team meetings, sales conferences, and product launches.	• These are ideal opportunities for generating motivation within the organization or team. • Functions can be expensive because they need careful planning, preparation, and follow-up. Larger events also often require professional help and first-class venues.
PUBLICATIONS Including glossy magazines and desktop-published news sheets.	• Take care to match publications to employees' likes, dislikes, and needs. Use research, such as inviting readers' comments, to ensure the effort is paying off. • These require a lot of effort for what may be low readership.
ELECTRONIC Including Web sites, intranets, and other electronic networks.	• The biggest advantage is that these can be updated continually and give an instant response to questions. Information can be sent worldwide in seconds. • The biggest drawback is potential abuse, including use for personal – not business – needs.
TELEVISUAL Including videos, closed-circuit TV, and multimedia.	• This is a fast-growing modern approach which often uses interactive elements for optimum effect. • These communication methods can be expensive because they require professional input and training.

TALKING UP THE TEAM

One of your responsibilities as a manager is the "advertising" of your team's image among peers and superiors. To do this, make sure you credit staff for their work, strive to have senior managers present at celebrations and in training or strategy sessions, make sure that good news about the department is covered in corporate journalism, and show off any inside achievements in outside presentations.

 98 Find out which colleagues are most skilled at communicating.

CHECKING YOUR MESSAGE GETS THROUGH

If you are communicating to improve perceptions, you need to check how your message is received. Managers are often very bad judges of this. Remember there is only one reliable source of information on perceptions: the recipients of the messages.

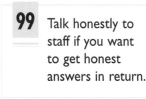

99 Talk honestly to staff if you want to get honest answers in return.

EVALUATING PERCEPTIONS

The acid test of whether internal and external communications are successful is what the recipients perceive. An unfavourable perception is either merited, or the intended message did not get through. Whichever the case, you must take action. Honest analysis of the reasons will provide a basis for effective communication in future.

GETTING ▼ USEFUL FEEDBACK

How feedback is transmitted, and what happens in response to it, is basic to effective communication. Always act promptly when you get feedback. Also, hold team meetings regularly to check that feedback is well used.

LISTENING TO STAFF

The most important feedback is in individual, informal conversations between managers and those managed. However, you can also check how management is perceived by using a more formal approach, such as conducting attitude surveys, although these are sometimes expensive to carry out. Other ways to get useful information include more limited surveys, sample polling, suggestion boxes, and focus groups. For example, try polling your employees twice yearly to discover how they rate management. Targeted enquiries like this will raise issues, and give more general indications of morale. As with all feedback, what matters most is how you respond to what you hear.

QUESTIONS TO ASK STAFF

Q How do you get most of your information about the organization?

Q Does your manager communicate with you constantly, often, sometimes, or hardly ever?

Q What do you understand about the company's strategy?

Q What would you like to know that you are not told?

Q Which type of communication is most effective for you?

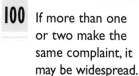

100 If more than one or two make the same complaint, it may be widespread.

GETTING OUTSIDE VIEWS

If problems are revealed by internal questionnaires or through focus groups, one-to-one employee interviews, or any other meetings, the chances are that the external perceptions of the company also need to be improved. Get feedback by talking to your suppliers, clients, and customers, or perhaps by conducting a survey of target groups. Also, check the general response to recent advertising or PR campaigns. If the feedback suggests any dissatisfaction, you need to find remedies fast.

IMPROVING COMMUNICATION

To improve internal communications, involve all managers, stressing their responsibility for communicating clearly and consistently at all times. Decide whether other staff also need to improve their communication skills. For external communications, agree a plan of action with all the relevant people. You must get to the root of any problem, strengthen your effectiveness, and shift perceptions, or mistakes will be repeated.

101 If you get only positive feedback, it may well not be the whole truth.

ASSESSING YOUR COMMUNICATION SKILLS

Evalute how well you communicate by responding to the following statements. Mark the options that are closest to your experience. Be as honest as you can: if your answer is "never", mark Option 1; if it is "always", mark Option 4; and so on. Add your scores together, and refer to the Analysis to see how skilled you are at communicating. Use your answers to identify the areas that need improvement.

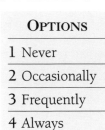

OPTIONS

1 Never

2 Occasionally

3 Frequently

4 Always

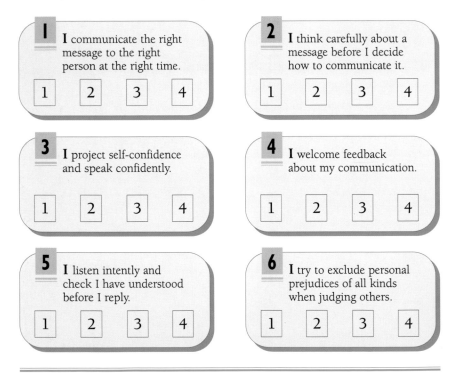

1 I communicate the right message to the right person at the right time.

1 2 3 4

2 I think carefully about a message before I decide how to communicate it.

1 2 3 4

3 I project self-confidence and speak confidently.

1 2 3 4

4 I welcome feedback about my communication.

1 2 3 4

5 I listen intently and check I have understood before I reply.

1 2 3 4

6 I try to exclude personal prejudices of all kinds when judging others.

1 2 3 4

7 I am constructive and civil when I meet others.

1   2   3   4

8 I take time to give people the information they need and want.

1   2   3   4

9 I use one-to-one meetings for reviews of performance and coaching.

1   2   3   4

10 I question people to find out what they think and how they are getting on.

1   2   3   4

11 I hand out written briefs that give all pertinent information on a task.

1   2   3   4

12 I use professional phone techniques to improve my communication.

1   2   3   4

13 I communicate via all available electronic media.

1   2   3   4

14 I apply the rules of good writing to external and internal communications.

1   2   3   4

15 I use an effective system of note-taking for minutes, interviews, and research.

1   2   3   4

16 I test important letters and documents on reliable critics before finalizing.

1   2   3   4

17 I use fast reading techniques to speed up my work rate.

1   2   3   4

18 I prepare speeches carefully and deliver them well after rehearsal.

1   2   3   4

19 I take an active and highly visible role in internal training.

1   2   3   4

20 I plan important events, such as conferences, to high professional standards.

1   2   3   4

21 I apply the rules of soft and hard selling to put across my points of view.

1   2   3   4

22 I enter negotiations fully primed on issues and on the other side's needs.

1   2   3   4

23 I make my reports accurate, concise, clear, and well structured.

1   2   3   4

24 I research thoroughly before putting forward a written proposal.

1   2   3   4

25 I try to understand how all relevant audiences react to the organization.

1   2   3   4

26 I consider how skilled advisers can help on public relations issues.

1   2   3   4

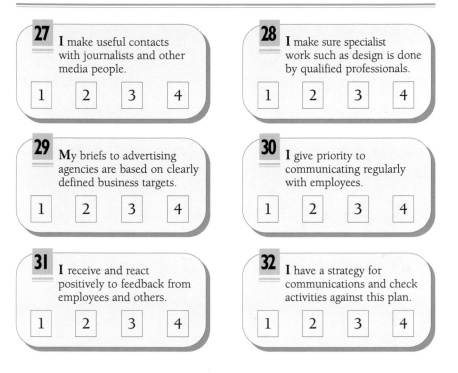

27 I make useful contacts with journalists and other media people.

| 1 | 2 | 3 | 4 |

28 I make sure specialist work such as design is done by qualified professionals.

| 1 | 2 | 3 | 4 |

29 My briefs to advertising agencies are based on clearly defined business targets.

| 1 | 2 | 3 | 4 |

30 I give priority to communicating regularly with employees.

| 1 | 2 | 3 | 4 |

31 I receive and react positively to feedback from employees and others.

| 1 | 2 | 3 | 4 |

32 I have a strategy for communications and check activities against this plan.

| 1 | 2 | 3 | 4 |

ANALYSIS

Now you have completed the self-assessment, add up your total score and check your performance by reading the corresponding evaluation. Whatever level of success you have achieved when communicating, it is important to remember that there is always room for improvement. Identify your weakest areas, and refer to the sections in this book where you will find practical advice and tips to help you to hone your communication skills.

32–64: You are not communicating effectively or enough. Listen to feedback, and try to learn from your mistakes.
65–95: Your communications performance is patchy. Plan to improve your weaknesses.
96–128: You communicate extremely well. But remember that you can never communicate too much.

INDEX